BIBLE 101

SIX SESSIONS FOR SMALL GROUPS

PARABLES & PROPHECY

Unlocking the Bible's mysteries

GW00674338

WILLOW CREEK RESOURCES

BILL DONAHUE

BILL DONAHUE, SERIES EDITOR

IVP

InterVarsity Press
Downers Grove, Illinois
Leicester, England

InterVarsity Press
P.O. Box 1400, Downers Grove, IL 60515
World Wide Web: www.ivpress.com
E-mail: mail@ivpress.com

Inter-Varsity Press, England
38 De Montfort Street, Leicester LE1 7GP, England

InterVarsity Press® is the book-publishing division of InterVarsity Christian Fellowship/USA®, a student movement active on campus at hundreds of universities, colleges and schools of nursing in the United States of America, and a member movement of the International Fellowship of Evangelical Students. For information about local and regional activities, write Public Relations Dept., InterVarsity Christian Fellowship/USA, 6400 Schroeder Rd., P.O. Box 7895, Madison, WI 53707-7895.

Inter-Varsity Press, England, is the book-publishing division of the Universities and Colleges Christian Fellowship (formerly the Inter-Varsity Fellowship), a student movement linking Christian Unions in universities and colleges throughout the United Kingdom and the Republic of Ireland, and a member movement of the International Fellowship of Evangelical Students. For information about local and national activities write to UCCF, 38 De Montfort Street, Leicester LE1 7GP.

All Scripture quotations, unless otherwise indicated, are taken from the Holy Bible, New International Version®. NIV®. Copyright ©1973, 1978, 1984 by International Bible Society. Used by permission of Zondervan Publishing House. All rights reserved. Distributed in the U.K. by permission of Hodder and Stoughton Ltd. All rights reserved. "NIV" is a registered trademark of International Bible Society. UK trademark number 1448790.

Cover design: Grey Matter Group

Photo image: Michael VanderKallen

Chapter icon: Roberta Polfus

USA ISBN 0-8308-2066-3

UK ISBN 0-85111-530-6

Printed in the United States of America ∞

15	14	13	12	11	10	9	8	7	6	5	4	3	2	1
11	10	09	08	07	06	05	04	03	02	01	00			

Contents

Introduction

Some time ago, Russ Robinson (director of small group ministries at Willow Creek Community Church and concept editor on these guides) and I were talking about how to help groups get a firm grip on the Word of God. Both of us had studied and taught courses on the Bible, but what about small groups? What if we could put something together that could be studied as a group and yet have much of the information people would normally find in a class or course? Well, hats off to Russ, who came up with the idea for Bible 101 and cast the vision for what it could look like. Soon we were outlining the books and the result is what you have before you. So welcome to the Bible 101 adventure, a place where truth meets life!

Traditionally the subject matter in this series has been reserved for classroom teaching or personal study. Both are places where this curriculum could be used. But this work is primarily targeted at small groups, places where men and women, old and young, rich and poor gather together in community to engage fully with the truth of God's Word. These little communities can be transforming in ways that classrooms and personal study cannot.

Few things in life are more fulfilling than drawing out the deep truths of Scripture and then seeing them at work to change a life into the image of Christ. Getting a firm grip on the Bible and its teachings is paramount to a mature and intelligent walk with God. We are to worship him with all our heart, soul, mind and strength. And the Word of God is central to accomplishing God's desire that we be fully devoted to him.

The team from Willow Creek—staff and volunteers alike—has labored diligently to provide you with a group-friendly process for understanding the Bible. Kathy Dice, Gerry Mathisen, Judson Poling, Michael Redding and I have worked to provide something that merges content and process, learning and application. Now it is up to you to work together to discover the riches that lie ahead for those willing to do some work and take a few risks. But we know you are more than ready for that challenge!

To make these studies more productive, here are a few suggestions and guidelines to help you along the way. Read carefully so that you get the most out of this series.

Purpose

This series is designed to ground a Christ-follower in the study and understanding of Scripture. It is not designed for someone who became a Christian last week, though sections of it would certainly be good. And it is not as rigorous as a Bible college class or seminary course might be. Bible 101 means *foundational,* but not easy or light. So be prepared for some challenge and some stretching. This may be the first time you are exposed to certain theological concepts or terms, or to some more in-depth methods of Bible study. Celebrate the challenge and strive to do your best. Peter tells us to "make every effort" to add knowledge to our faith. It will take some effort, but I can guarantee it will be well worth it!

Prayer

When approaching the Word of God you will need to keep a submissive and teachable attitude. The Holy Spirit is eager to teach you, but you must be willing to receive knowledge, encouragement, correction and challenge. One educator has taught that all learning is the result of failed expectations. We hope that in some ways you are ambushed by the truth and stumble upon new and unfamiliar territory that startles you into new ways of thinking about God and relating to him through Christ.

Practice

Each session has the same format, except (in some cases) the last session. For five meetings you will learn skills, discuss material and readings, work together as a team, and discover God's truths in fresh and meaningful ways. The sixth session will be an opportunity to put all you have learned into practice. Studies are designed as follows.

 Establishing Base Camp (5-10 minutes). A question or icebreaker to focus the meeting.

Mapping the Trail (5-10 minutes). An overview of where we are headed.

 Beginning the Ascent (30 minutes). The main portion of the discussion time.

Gaining a Foothold (3 minutes). Information to read that identifies core issues and ideas to keep you on track with the journey.

 Trailmarkers (10 minutes). Important Scriptures for memorization or reflection.

 Teamwork (15 minutes). A group activity (sometimes done in subgroups) to build community and share understanding of what was learned.

 Reaching the Summit (5 minutes). A chance to summarize and look back at what has been learned or accomplished.

Close in Prayer (as long as you want!). An opportunity to pray for one another and ask God to deepen the truths of Scripture in you.

You can take some shortcuts or take longer as the group decides, but strive to stay on schedule for a 75- to 90-minute meeting, including prayer time. You will also want to save time to attend to personal needs. This will vary by group and can also be accomplished in personal relationships you develop between meetings.

Preparation

Preparation? There is none! Well, almost none. For some sessions reading ahead will be suggested to provide an overview. But the sessions are designed to be worked through together. We find this builds a sense of team and community, and is also more fun! And there is something about "discovery in the moment" rather than merely discussing what everyone has already discovered outside the meeting that provides a sense of adventure.

We wish you the best as you draw truth from the Word of God for personal transformation, group growth and kingdom impact!

Bill Donahue, Series Editor
Vice President, Small Group Ministries
Willow Creek Assocation

Session 1

Experiencing a Psalm

Getting the most out of reading Hebrew poetry.

Establishing Base Camp

Poetry does not often find its way onto the *New York Time*'s Bestseller List. Viewed sometimes as too sophisticated, as in "How do I love thee? Let me count the ways," or too simple, as in "Mary had a little lamb," poetry captures our hearts and moves our souls.

Sometimes poems are lighthearted. One Christmas Eve I read the full version of *The Night Before Christmas* by Clement Clarke Moore to my son, who is a few years past the Santa Claus stage. We laughed and smiled as the words captured our imaginations and painted images of the mythical jolly old Saint Nick. Somehow the poem captured the moment more than any other story could.

More serious poems are written about times of great loss or death. Walt Whitman's "O Captain, My Captain," made famous again in the movie *Dead Poet's Society,* describes the death of a man's father, his "Captain," as he lies in his arms. Others are born out of times of great struggle or crisis, when we are faced with the realities of life and death, of God and eternity. One of my favorites has always been "Trees" by Sergeant Joyce Kilmer of the 165th Infantry in World War I.

I think that I shall never see
A poem lovely as a tree.

A tree whose hungry mouth is prest
Against the earth's sweet flowing breast;

A tree that looks at God all day,
And lifts her leafy arms to pray;

A tree that may in summer wear
A nest of robins in her hair;

Upon whose bosom snow has lain;
Who intimately lives with rain.

Poems are made by fools like me,
But only God can make a tree.

Like King David, Kilmer was a soldier, poet and leader. A man full of emotion and with a keen sense of how to capture the deepest thoughts with the simplest words and images. I picture him in a trench in France covered in mud, deprived of shelter, under attack from the enemy and longing to be home. In the face of all this, he has his God and his poetry. His soul is centered and his faith simple yet profound.

✓ **Is there a poem, nursery rhyme or childhood song you heard when you were young that still sticks with you today? What do you remember about it and what memories does it bring?**

Mapping the Trail

Hebrew poetry, found in great measure in Psalms, Proverbs, Song of Songs and many prophetic books, is far different from our Western poetry. Most poems we are familiar with are structured using rhyme and meter (a steady tempo). Hebrew poetry is structured with parallelisms—ideas that "rhyme" rather than words that sound alike. And there is much imagery. Word pictures are created to move the reader. And much biblical poetry is set to music (particularly in the Psalms).

Leland Ryken, in *How to Read the Bible as Literature,* describes various types of parallelism. Here are a few major ones:

Synonymous: Where two statements say the same thing, reinforcing a truth or idea.

The heavens declare the glory of God;
    the skies proclaim the work of his hands. (Psalm 19:1)

Antithetic: Where the second line restates the truth of the first line, but in an opposite or negative way.

For the LORD watches over the way of the righteous,
   but the way of the wicked will perish. (Psalm 1:6)

Climactic: Where the second statement builds on the first, often repeating it and then adding to it.

Ascribe to the LORD, O mighty ones,
   ascribe to the LORD glory and strength. (Psalm 29:1)

Synthetic: Where the lines form a complete unit, one idea building on another to make a complete thought.

The wicked freely strut about
   when what is vile is honored among men. (Psalm 12:8)

It is not important that you memorize the names of these parallelisms. But it is important to recognize them in your reading of Psalms because it will help you interpret them. The words in parallelism, says Ryken, "enhance each other" and say powerfully what neither part could say on its own.

Beginning the Ascent

The psalms use emotions and imagery to convey truthful doctrine and feelings. The psalms are our prayer guide and indeed served as a prayer and worship manual for the Hebrews and the early Christians. Look at these opening statements in Psalms and feel the emotion of the writer.

The Emotions of the Psalms

Despair
How long, O LORD? Will you forget me forever?
   How long will you hide your face from me?
   (Psalm 13:1)

Celebration
O LORD, the king rejoices in your strength.
   How great is his joy in the victories you give!
   (Psalm 21:1)

"The effect of parallelism is comparable to turning a prism in the light, insuring that we will look at the colors of a statement at least twice. Needless to say, this accords perfectly with the meditative purpose of the Bible and the nature of poetic language." (Leland Ryken, *How to Read the Bible as Literature*)

Confidence
> To you, O LORD, I lift up my soul;
>> in you I trust, O my God. (Psalm 25:1)

Fear
> Save me, O God, by your name;
>> vindicate me by your might.
> Hear my prayer, O God;
>> listen to the words of my mouth. (Psalm 54:1-2)

Anger
> May God arise, may his enemies be scattered;
>> may his foes flee before him.
> As smoke is blown away by the wind,
>> may you blow them away;
> as wax melts before the fire,
>> may the wicked perish before God. (Psalm 68:1-2)

These are some tough words. Often we sing the praise portion of psalms in worship services. But those last two psalms were written to be sung by choirs—imagine that as the offertory hymn next week at your church!

Also notice the use of images in Psalm 68. Smoke, wind, wax and fire create a memorable picture of the judgment of God that David so desperately seeks for his enemies. In this case it is a victory song, but Psalm 54 is an outright plea for the destruction of people trying to kill David.

✓ **What strikes you about David's words as he speaks to God and writes his poetry?**

✓ **David, who wrote almost half of the Psalms, appeared to have the freedom to express his full emotions and desires to God. What keeps us from doing the same?**

The most important function of the Psalms is to draw us to God.

According to the *Revell Bible Dictionary:* "Essentially, the theology of the psalms is relational. The psalms draw attention to the relationship with God experienced by his people as they pass through this life. [They] model intimacy with God and show us how to relate any situation in which we may find ourselves to the Lord."

In speaking of the power of the Psalms, the *New Bible Dictionary* states, "Here are mirrored the ideals of religious piety and communion with God ... of obedience to the law of God, delight in the worship of God, fellowship with the friends of God, reverence for the Word of God."

Types of Psalms

Psalms are poems put to music and were written to serve varied situations, the purpose of the writer and the truth God is communicating to his people. So we should expect the psalms to take various forms. Here are the most common types of psalms.

Lament: This is the largest group of psalms (there are over sixty laments), and it typically includes a cry to God, a description of the crisis, a request for help, a statement of confidence in God and praise to God. Psalm 54, mentioned above, is a lament. Laments may be personal (Psalms 13; 22; 39), while still others are corporate (Psalms 12; 44; 80).

Thanksgiving: Many Psalms (90—105, 107—117 and 135—150) would be in this group and are designed to give adoration and thanks to God for who he is and what he has done.

Individual praise: Psalms 11, 18, 23, 46 and others reveal the heart of an individual as God is lifted up and given honor.

History of redemption: These five psalms (78; 105; 106; 135; 136) focus on Israel's deliverance from bondage and Israel as a chosen people.

Wisdom: Psalms 36, 37, 112, 127 are examples of psalms that read almost like proverbs (wisdom sayings). Proverbs 8, which incidentally personifies wisdom, is a psalm of sorts.

Penitential: These are psalms of confession and forgiveness. Psalms 32, 51 and 130 are the best-known.

Messianic: Psalms 2, 22 and 110 are the most commonly referred to psalms that speak of the Christ, the Messiah.

Gaining a Foothold

Gordon Fee and Douglas Stuart, in their book *How to Read the Bible for All Its Worth*, outline three benefits we gain from reading Psalms.
1. They provide a guide to worship: these songs provide us with the words to say for any occasion as we recognize who God is and what he has done for us.
2. They demonstrate how to relate honestly to God: anger, fear, joy and sorrow are all expressed to God in the Psalms.
3. They invite us to reflection and meditation on God; it is difficult not to think deeply when reading these powerful words.

Trailmarkers

Here's a real challenge. Psalm 1 is the entryway to the entire psalter. It focuses on meditation and obedience of the Word of God and sets the stage for a life of worship, reflection and trust in God. Get a partner and try to memorize as much of this psalm as possible. Especially concentrate on verses 1-3. Many believers through the ages have found it worth meditating on and coming back to over and over for assurance and spiritual strength.

Teamwork

Dig into Psalm 1. First, look at each verse and identify the kind of parallelism it is. Is it synonymous? antithetic? climactic? synthetic?

Verse 1 _____

Verse 2 _____

Verse 3 _____

Verse 4 _____

Verse 5 _____

Verse 6 _____

Second, what kind of psalm is it? lament? thanksgiving? wisdom? praise?

Third, what imagery does it use, and how does that help you understand the meaning of the psalm?

How has God spoken to you using this psalm?

 Reaching the Summit

The Psalms are a rich resource for relating to and understanding God. Knowing the type of psalm, the setting from which it was written, the emotions expressed and the basic parallel format will help you interpret the psalm accurately and hear the message of God powerfully.

✓ How has this study of the Psalms affected your appreciation of them as poetic literature and as scriptural truth?

Next Session

Read Proverbs 1:1-7 and list the benefits of wisdom. Next time we will take a look at an often-misunderstood form of biblical literature—the proverb.

Old Chinese proverb: He who thinks he leads but has no one following, is only taking a walk.

Close in Prayer

Thank God for what you have learned about worship from the Psalms. Consider praying through a psalm together that expresses what you are learning.

Session 2

Applying a Proverb

Finding guidance for life in the book of wisdom sayings.

Establishing Base Camp

I grew up in Philadelphia, Pennsylvania, a city packed with history. A prominent figure in Philadelphia was Benjamin Franklin, known for his many inventions and keen wit. Though many of his sayings had a humorous bent, others contained a wisdom learned over the years. Here are a few from his works *Maxims and Morals* and *Poor Richard's Almanac:*

Without virtue man can have no happiness.
God heals, and the doctor takes the fees.
Search others for their virtues, thyself for thy vices.
Keep your eyes open before marriage, half shut afterwards.
God helps them that help themselves.

From sages to elders to learned teachers, wisdom is passed along from generation to generation. Some of it is sound and practical, some falls into the category of superstition. (Break a mirror and you'll have seven years bad luck.)

✓ Who in your life has been a source of wisdom?

✓ Why do you seek that person for counsel and advice?

Mapping the Trail

Though you might argue that wise teaching is found throughout the Bible, the wisdom books traditionally are Job, Proverbs and Ecclesiastes. These writings of the Old Testament provide the reader with insight for decision-making and quality relationships.

Wisdom literature in the Bible can be summed up as providing "skill for living." The sayings of these three books make available to readers the lessons learned by those who have preceded us. The book of Proverbs is the most popular and is filled with wise sayings and warnings. The purpose of the book is "to give prudence to the simple, knowledge and discretion to the young" (1:4) and make those who are wise even more wise (1:5).

✓ Read Proverbs 1:1-7. What are the benefits of wisdom?

✓ How does this relate to our walk with God?

Beginning the Ascent

You have probably heard the proverb "Train a child in the way he should go, and when he is old he will not turn from it" (22:6). Yet many of us have questioned this. *But the Johnson's sent Billy to a Christian school, had family devotions, prayed for their son and lived a faithful life. Why did Billy rebel against them and God? Doesn't the Bible say if we train them they will never depart from God's way?* This question could obviously have many answers; we don't know all the family dynamics in any given situation. But two things are clear: (1) We are all responsible for our own actions, and (2) we cannot treat a *proverb* the same as a *promise.*

Proverbs are wisdom sayings. All things being equal, and without extenuating circumstances, they are true. Proverbs give us general principles for wise living. They are not timeless promises applied to each and every circumstance in life. For example, look at Proverbs 22:29: "Do you see a man skilled in his work? He will serve before kings; he will not serve before obscure men."

Does this mean that everyone who performs their work skillfully will be hired onto the staff of a king? Is every skilled person working for an "obscure" man or woman deceived? Maybe they really aren't that skilled! If they were, they'd be working in a palace.

Obviously there is a different meaning. But how do we get at that meaning? A timeless promise ("I will never leave you nor forsake you") applies to every believer in every circumstance. But a proverb applies to most circumstances and most people. The book of Proverbs is a guideline for living, not a promise book. Wisdom in general is to be treated this way.

✓ Consider the following wisdom of the world. Should it be applied in all circumstances? Describe any exceptions you see.

1. "Early to bed, early to rise, makes a man healthy, wealthy and wise."

2. "Look before you leap."

3. "A penny saved is a penny earned."

4. "The pen is mightier than the sword."

Guidelines for Understanding Proverbs

The following guidelines, adapted from *How to Read the Bible for All Its Worth* by Gordon Fee and Douglas Stuart, will guard the student of the Bible from misinterpreting and misapplying this wisdom for living.

Consider the context. Proverbs 9:17 says, "Stolen water is sweet; food eaten in secret is delicious!" Is that what the Bible teaches? If we look at the preceding verses, we see that this is not the voice of Wisdom recorded in Proverbs 9:1-12. This is the voice of Folly (the wayward, rebellious life), which speaks beginning in verse 13. Note that verse 18 says, "But little do they know that the dead are there, that her (Folly, that is) guests are in the depths of the grave." The context here is the lifestyle of the fool contrasted with that of the wise.

> "No proverb is a complete statement of truth. No proverb is so perfectly worded that it can stand up to the unreasonable demand that it apply in every situation at every time." (*How to Read the Bible for all Its Worth*, **Gordon Fee & Douglas Stuart**)

Proverbs are not promises. The rewards and blessings often mentioned in Proverbs are likely to follow the action taken, but this is not guaranteed. Look at Proverbs 10:4: "Lazy hands make a man poor, but diligent hands bring wealth."

You've probably heard of some lazy couple that won an illegitimate lawsuit for millions, yet you have a friend who has worked hard but his company just got downsized and he's been out of work for months. This is not a promise. It is a wise principle and generally holds true.

Proverbs must be read as a collection. Proverbs must be balanced against one another and be taken into the context of the entire Scripture. For example, look at Proverbs 6:20: "My son, keep your father's commands and do not forsake your mother's teaching."

Does this apply to the son at all times? What if the teaching is clearly wrong or unwise? The use of common sense and the clear teaching of Scripture about the relationship of children to parents will provide a better framework for interpretation. The verses that follow this proverb merely affirm that parents have much wisdom, in this case it is wisdom that will keep the son from falling into the hands of a prostitute.

Proverbs uses the allegory of a parent and a son for communication purposes. The writer creates a dialogue of sorts so that we hear the voice of Wisdom speaking to us in a direct and personal way. In other cases Wisdom is personified as a woman, and we are told to listen to her carefully. This is a literary device, not intended to be the actual conversation between a parent and child.

Proverbs are designed to be more memorable than accurate. Proverbs are pithy sayings designed so that they are remembered. For example, we already listed the common "look before you leap" proverb. Fee and Stuart suggest that this saying is memorable but not accurate in every circumstance. They point out that it sure beats saying, "In advance of committing yourself to a course of action, consider your circumstances and options." Covering every possible exception and circumstance is too complex and is quickly forgotten. What is more important is that the wise saying is easily retained.

Some proverbs must be translated to be understood. Look again at Proverbs 22:29. We don't live in a society with kings. Instead, the "king" here is intended to be representative of all leaders. The purpose of the proverb is to show that those who work hard and become highly skilled in their work will be admired and sought after by people in leadership. This is true today. The principle behind the proverb remains as true as it did in Solomon's day.

Another example is Proverbs 31:10-31. Few women (if any) fit the full description of this most excellent wife. The writer, using a device called "hyperbole," is exaggerating to make a point. (It is also an acrostic poem in Hebrew, each line beginning with a successive letter of the Hebrew alphabet.) Jesus used hyperbole when he said, "If your right eye causes you to sin, gouge it out and throw it away. It is better to lose one part of your body than for your whole body to be thrown into hell" (Matthew 5:29).

Proverbs 31 can be translated in this way: "This is how a godly woman goes about her life. If she has children, she cares for them with proper clothing. When she works, she works diligently, making sacrifices if necessary to support her family. She is resourceful and seeks to make wise decisions. If she is in the marketplace, she seeks to build her business with integrity and profitability."

This passage is not intended to make a woman feel guilty for not being all things mentioned. Rather, this is a composite woman, an ideal that can be aspired to depending on each woman's station in life, resources, number of children, income level (this woman has servants!) and physical ability. It shows how much impact a woman devoted to God can make on her family and the world.

Take a moment to reflect on what has been discussed. What has become more clear or understandable about your study of proverbs and how to interpret them accurately?

Gaining a Foothold

When applying a proverb, remember:
- A proverb is a form of poetic literature that uses imagery to convey a truth.
- A proverb is not a timeless promise; it is a wisdom saying.
- Proverbs must be taken in context with an understanding of the setting.
- Proverbs are worded to be pithy and memorable, not comprehensive for all situations.
- Proverbs must be read as a collection, not in isolation.
- Some proverbs require translation across cultures to get at the wisdom being described.

Trailmarkers

Here are two key passages from Proverbs to center you on the purpose of the book and the value of wisdom literature in general. Reflect on these in teams or with a partner. Try memorizing one of them this week. If you have a moment, get started now.

Proverbs 1:7: "The fear of the LORD is the beginning of knowledge, but fools despise wisdom and discipline."

Proverbs 3:13-14: "Blessed is the man who finds wisdom, the man who gains understanding, for she is more profitable than silver and yields better returns than gold."

Teamwork

Read Proverbs 24:30-34. This passage covers just about every aspect of a proverb. In small groups or teams, unpack this proverb using what you have learned. Here are some questions to which you can apply the guidelines we have been discussing. See "Gaining a Foothold" for a review.

1. What images are being created by the writer?

2. Identify the kind of parallelism in each verse (synonymous, antithetic, climactic or synthetic).

3. How does the writer use exaggeration (hyperbole) to make his point?

4. What is being emphasized here? What is the wisdom principle?

5. What is not being emphasized? (For example, is sleep bad?)

Reaching the Summit

So many people read Proverbs in their devotions but misapply them or lack the ability to understand them. This causes frustration and sometimes disappointment with God for "breaking a promise" and not living up to expectations.

✓ How has this study brought clarity or perhaps even relief to you regarding your understanding of Proverbs?

Next Session

Prophetic literature is about the most intimidating aspect of the Bible for most people. We are often forced to rely on someone else's interpretation and find we have few resources of our own to give us any confidence. The next session will give you the guidelines you need for basic study of prophetic literature in the Bible. In preparation, bring an example of a prophecy that failed to come true. It can be on paper or simply one you have heard.

Close in Prayer

Thank God for the deposit of wisdom he has made in our lives. If we heed it, we can be assured that in most cases we will benefit by making wiser choices and avoiding foolish mistakes.

Session 3

Deciphering a Prophecy

Discovering how God uses prophecy to shape us into Christ's image.

Establishing Base Camp

Images are powerful. Photographs, special effects in movies and artwork are used to create powerful emotions and profound thoughts. This struck me most powerfully at my parents' fiftieth wedding anniversary.

Thanks to the creativity of my wife (and some hard work by all of us) we presented my parents with a series of gifts—poems, songs, toasts—that unveiled memories and highlighted my parents' unfailing love. The most impressive of these was a display at the receiving line, where friends could catch a glimpse of their fifty years together. World War II medals, awards, lockets and assorted memorabilia were scattered in front of a photo collage depicting defining moments and meaningful relationships. I'll never forget the impression I had as the lives of two people were captured visually in that one moment, right before my eyes. I was very moved as I pondered all they had done and experienced.

✓ Describe a photo, a scene from a movie or a piece of artwork that has had a lasting impact on your life. How has it influenced you?

Mapping the Trail

Biblical prophecy is a much maligned and misused form of literature. As much as one-third of the Bible could be classified as prophetic or apocalyptic literature, and we should be wise in how we handle it (see 2 Timothy 2:15).

✓ What comes to mind when you think of Bible prophecy?

✓ How have prophecies and prophetic teachings been useful to the church?

✓ How have they been abused?

In this session we'll discover tools for reading and understanding prophecy.

Beginning the Ascent

A prophecy is simply a word from God to his people. It can come in the mode of *foretelling* the future or in *forthtelling* a set of judgments or exhortations. In most cases it is a call to return to God's covenant and laws. In some cases it may also be predictive of future events. In any case, when a prophecy was given to Israel or to the church, it was to be taken as God's word for the people to hear and obey.

Notice how Jeremiah was called on to speak the very words of God to the people. His prophecies were truths from the Father to be given to his children: "The LORD said to me, 'Do not say, "I am only a child." You must go to everyone I send you to and say whatever I command you.' . . . Then the LORD reached out his hand and touched my mouth and said to me, 'Now I have put my words in your mouth'" (Jeremiah 1:7, 9).

It should also be noted that most Old Testament prophecy was fulfilled either during Old Testament history or in Christ. Though there are prophecies yet to be realized concerning the second coming, we look to the clear and direct teaching of the Scripture (particularly the New Testament) for guidance on how to live our Christian lives. We are not waiting for God to speak through a new prophet, because we have his Holy Spirit in us to teach and guide us, and we have the Scriptures. The Old Testament believer did not have the resources we have today.

The Role of a Prophet

In the Old Testament period there were three main leadership roles in Israel—prophet, priest and king. The king was to be God's representative for carrying out justice and maintaining peace, the priest interceded on behalf of the people to God, and the prophet spoke on behalf of God to the people. Old Testament prophets were God's spokespersons, pointing out national sins, confronting and counseling kings, and calling nations to repentance.

Most prophetic activity took place between 800 B.C. and 430 B.C. This is primarily because rebellion, social disorder, civil war and religious apostasy characterized this period in Israel's history. Prophets were sent to call God's people back to him (or face God's righteous wrath).

In the New Testament, prophets played a less significant role for several reasons. First, because John the Baptist is said to be the last of the great Old Testament prophets (Matthew 14:11-15). Second, the work of the prophets was fulfilled in Christ's coming. Third, since Christ is the full revelation of the Father (Hebrews 1:1-3), there is little that the prophets can tell us that Christ and the apostles have not already said (Ephesians 2:20).

So what is the role of the New Testament prophet? First we must distinguish between the role of a prophet and the gift of prophecy. There were prophets in the time of the early church (for example, Agabus in Acts 11:28 and Philip's four daughters in Acts 21:9). Prophets were given to the church along with pastors, teachers and others to strengthen the church (1 Corinthians 14:29-32; Ephesians 4:11). Their role appears to be a ministry of exhortation, calling the church to obedience, truth and repentance. New Testament prophets—except for Jesus—make few predictive prophecies that have been recorded.

The gift of prophecy as described in 1 Corinthians 12—14 is useful to the church for edification. But it was also regulated and did not appear to be on the same authoritative level as Old Testament prophecy. Notice that Paul encourages the congregation to "weigh carefully what is said" when a prophet speaks

(14:29), implying a prophecy might be off-target. Other prophets were to evaluate a prophecy to see if it had bearing on the life of the church (14:32). This was never true of Old Testament prophets who spoke the authoritative word of God. These words were to be obeyed, not discussed.

How do you distinguish a false prophet from a true one? Look at Deuteronomy 13:1-5 and 18:14-22, and answer these questions.

✔ What is the purpose of a prophet?

✔ How were God's people to distinguish between true and false prophets?

✔ What was the penalty for a false prophet who claimed to speak for God?

Prophecy as Literature
Here are the basic categories of prophecy and examples of each. Look up the verses cited to get a feel for the different types of prophecy.

Predictive (foretelling). To reveal future events (judgments, consequences for sin, victories) so that people would be moved to action that honors God. Most prophetic predictions were fulfilled in the Old Testament or by the time of Christ. There are some that still require fulfillment, mostly related to the second coming of Jesus.

✔ Read Isaiah 9:6-7 and 11:1-3 concerning the coming of Jesus as Messiah.

Exhortation (forthtelling). To speak forth the word of God and call people to obedience or repentance.

✓ Read Ezekiel 34:1-10 and note the tone of the passage.

Visionary (apocalyptic). Uses strong images and powerful drama to convey impending catastrophe or judgment, or to provide a picture of the future. As Leland Ryken says in *How to Read the Bible as Literature,* "visionary literature takes us to a strange world where ordinary rules of reality no longer prevail" (p. 166).

✓ Look at Revelation 1:12-16 for a description of Jesus Christ in visionary terms. The figures of speech are symbolic of Christ's character and provide a much more memorable image than simply saying, "He functions as our high priest and is pure and holy. He speaks the truth and should be respected and honored at all times." However, the symbols are not designed to be a picture of what he looks like in glory (see pullout quote).

> "Symbolic writing does not paint pictures. It is not pictographic but ideographic. The skull and crossbones on the bottle of medicine is a symbol of poison, not a picture. The fish, the lamb, and the lion are all symbols of Christ, but never to be taken as pictures of him. In other words, the symbol is a code word and does not paint a picture." (Donald Richardson, quoted in *How to Read the Bible as Literature* by Leland Ryken)

Ground Rules for Interpreting Prophecy
1. Notice the context in which the passage is found. What is happening?
2. Find out if the historical context or setting sheds light on the prophecy.
3. Determine whether the prophecy is predictive, exhortation or visionary.
4. If predictive, how much of the prophecy has already been fulfilled?
5. Analyze the figures of speech used, if any.
6. Discern how it applied to the original audience and how much applies to the present time.
7. Does any of this point to Christ? Check cross-references for New Testament passages that apply.

Also consult commentaries and Bible dictionaries for help with terms, figures and possible interpretations.

(We will come back to these principles during the "Teamwork" portion of the session.)

Pitfalls to Avoid in Interpreting Prophecy

1. Be careful not to spiritualize the prophecy. Focus on the symbolism provided; do not add your own. Even though there is imagery used, it can

usually be understood by looking at the imagery in the historical and cultural context.

2. Don't narrow the scope of a prophecy. Some have an immediate fulfillment and a long-term one as well. One prophecy may have multiple fulfillments in history (see Acts 2:17-21 where not all of the prophecy has yet been completed).

3. Don't place more weight on an unclear or hard-to-understand prophecy than on the clear teaching of Scripture elsewhere. For example, you don't need to understand the vision in Revelation 4 in order to worship God fully. The psalms and the prayers of the Bible provide a great deal of information about the heart of a worshiper.

4. Don't apply a prophecy to your life that was intended specifically for others. You might learn from their experience, but don't take a prophecy out of context and assume it's given directly to you.

For example, read Jeremiah 29:11. In its context it refers specifically to the restoration of Israel from the seventy-year Babylonian captivity. Just three verses later the prophecy continues, "I will bring you back from captivity and gather you from all the nations and places where I have banished you." Verse 11 is often misapplied to individuals. Now, does this mean God has banished us as well? God was speaking of the great plans he had for his people after he rescued them from Babylon. There are other Scriptures that affirm God's love and his desires for all believers (Romans 8:32; Ephesians 3:14-21, for example). Better to quote them. God has great desires for us today, but that is not what Jeremiah 29:11 is teaching.

Gaining a Foothold

Three major approaches are often taken for interpreting Old Testament predictive prophecy. First, some deny the predictions, claiming that these were added to the text after the events actually occurred. Fortunately, the documentary evidence for Old Testament manuscripts does not support this. Others spiritualize the predictive elements and apply them symbolically. So, specific promises to Israel for land and peace are viewed as referring to the spiritual blessings all believers have in Christ. A third group assumes literal fulfillment of all prophecies, based on patterns of how earlier prophecies have already been fulfilled. You will come across all of these interpretative methods when you search commentaries for insights into a specific prophecy.

Trailmarkers

Here are two key passages to remember for clarity in prophecy: 1 Corinthians 14:29, 32 and 2 Peter 1:20-21.

The first emphasizes the role of the community in the understanding of any prophetic teaching or prophecy in the church.

The second reminds us that prophecy originates with the Holy Spirit and should therefore always reflect his character and be consistent with other teaching in the Word. Take a moment to discuss and memorize one of these passages.

Teamwork

Read Isaiah 52:13—53:12. See if you can gain perspective on this prophecy using the guidelines mentioned earlier. A study Bible would be beneficial, but for the sake of time we have provided some of the context and setting.

✔ Read the passage in blocks of three verses (stanzas); there are five of them. Focus on the main idea for each block, and do not get bogged down in details. If you want, divide into groups or pairs and divide these five sections among you.

52:13-15

53:1-3

53:4-6

53:7-9

53:10-12

This is the fourth of four "servant songs" in the book of Isaiah beginning in 42:1. Isaiah is describing the coming Suffering Servant who will redeem Israel. The time is approximately 670-680 B.C., and Isaiah has been sent to call the nation to repentance, warn of impending judgment on Israel and nations who have oppressed her, and promise ultimate restoration of the Jews and the coming of the Messiah. Consider the following questions.

What kind of prophecy is this?

What figures of speech are used?

How much of the prophecy is fulfilled?

What might apply to Israel here, and what applies to us?

What do you learn about God and his work from this passage?

Reaching the Summit

You have done well to tackle prophecy in just one session! You probably guessed that this is not enough, it but will give you some basic guidelines for reading prophetic literature. We encourage you to consult other wise believers, pastors and commentaries that will help you. There is great historical distance between a prophet's message and our time. (In the Isaiah prophecy above there is almost 2,700 years!) So it takes a lot of historical study and a Bible dictionary to help with names and figures of speech.

✓ Express to the group how you view prophecy now as a result of this session. Have any barriers been removed for understanding it? Are you still intimated by it?

Next Session

One of Jesus' greatest teaching tools was the parable. Read Matthew 13:11-16 where Jesus describes his reasons for using parables to teach. Come prepared to discuss this.

Close in Prayer

Praise God for his wisdom and thank him for the apostles and prophets on whom the foundation of the church is built. Their messages and visions have given us confidence that God will do what he has promised, and their words provide comfort as we look to the future when God will make all things right.

Session 4

Understanding a Parable

Interpreting and applying some of the most engaging teachings of Jesus.

Establishing Base Camp

For years now I have been the chief bedtime storyteller. I used to spin my tales of mystery to my son. From dinosaurs to space warriors, from Vikings to knights in armor, night after night we read or told stories that moved us to laughter and inspired us to heroic achievements (if only in our minds). Now that he's ten, he reads adventure books and biographies.

Lately, I have been fanning the flame of my daughter's imagination with stories of princesses, castles and giants (her idea—somehow she got into giants). The stories always have a moral—the triumph of good over evil or lessons learned as characters experience the consequences of their wise or foolish decisions. The kids love my stories and they remember most of them. My wife has encouraged me to write them in a book, but I am not sure I can capture the drama of the live event. We snuggle under the covers and I make things up as I go along, all to the fascination of the little treasure lying next to me.

✓ Think back to your childhood or even your early school years. What stories do you remember? How did they impact you?

Mapping the Trail

According to the *New Bible Dictionary*, "parable" is derived from the Greed word *parabolē*, ("putting things side by side"). It may take the form of a saying, proverb, story, simile or metaphor intended to communicate truth by comparison. Jesus often used parables to reveal life in the kingdom of God.

Jesus used stories to capture the minds of his listeners. These stories were mostly parables and were designed to convey truth to the open-hearted and to confuse the close-minded.

Take a moment to read Matthew 13:11-16. Why did Jesus teach in parables, a method that hides truth from some and reveals it to others?

 ## Beginning the Ascent

Parables are intended to be simple stories with profound implications for action. Yet at times even the most respected scholars and teachers have obscured the simple power of a parable by complicating or spiritualizing the elements of the story. Augustine, a theologian of the church in A.D. 400, interpreted the parable of the Good Samaritan from an allegorical viewpoint, assigning deep, hidden meanings to every component in the story. For Augustine, the man in the story represents Adam, the thieves are the devil and his angels, the Samaritan is Christ, the inn is the church, the money is the promise of life, and the innkeeper is Paul. Creative, but not what is intended in a parable!

Most parables are extended similes (a comparison using the words *like* or *as*). They often begin with "the kingdom of heaven is like" and focus on one key truth. Matthew 13 contains several parables that follow this pattern.

Parables are designed to call for a response to the truth that is revealed. It is not enough that the hearers understood a parable; Jesus expected them to "get the point" and do something about it. The details are there simply to help tell the story. We need not assign deeper meanings to specific details unless the context or the speaker demands that it be so. With this interpretive method we avoid the confusion created by mystical or allegorical approaches.

In contrast to visionary prophecy, where the images are often unfamiliar, parables use familiar images (such as wheat, seeds, vineyards, coins, bread) to reveal truths that are unfamiliar to the listener.

✓ Compare the images used in Revelation 4:6, "In the center, around the throne, were four living creatures, and they were covered with eyes, in front and in back," to the images in Matthew 13:31, "The kingdom of heaven is like a mustard seed, which a man took and planted in his field."

✓ Take a few moments to read the parable of the two sons in Matthew 20:28-32 and see if you can discern the central truth.

Principles for Interpreting the Parables

[from *Interpreting the Bible* by A. Berkeley Mickelsen]

1. Seek to *understand the "earthy details"* of the parable as the original hearers did. The elements of the story (mustard seeds, servants and oil lamps) are less familiar to us today in our urban cultures. We must familiarize ourselves with these details to understand the point of the story.

2. Note the *attitude and spiritual condition* of the audience.

3. When possible, *discern the reason that prompted Jesus* to employ the parable. Often it is a question or a challenge from cynics.

4. State concisely *the main point* of the parable.

5. Try to *relate the main point* of the parable to the basic components and core of Jesus' teaching (on the kingdom, for example).

6. Work hard to connect *the main emphasis* of the parable to current readers.

> "Jesus used parables to teach spiritual truths. The condition of each hearer determines whether the aim is realized or not. But Jesus used parables to throw light on the reign of God, on the demands of God, and on the response of men to the demands of God." (A. Berkeley Mickelsen, *Interpreting the Bible*)

Gaining a Foothold

When reading Jesus' parables keep the following in mind (condensed from *Revell Bible Dictionary*).

1. The kingdom of God is present when Christ or his people are present. Parables of the kingdom describe the reign of God in our lives.

2. There is a central issue that is relevant to the original hearers, usually in response to a question.

3. Not every element in a parable carries significance. Only those that address the issue under discussion are relevant.

4. To accurately interpret a parable you must understand the customs and culture of the main element in the parable.

Trailmarkers

Spiritual men and women can understand parables. But those without spiritual insight miss the point. Their hearts are hardened and rebellious.

Read 1 Corinthians 2:14 and commit it to memory: "The man [person] without the Spirit does not accept the things that come from the Spirit of God, for they are foolishness to him, and he cannot understand them, because they are spiritually discerned."

For context, read the larger passage of 2:6-16.

✓ Why is spiritual discernment so important in the church?

✓ Based on Jesus' comments in Matthew 13:15, what is required for spiritual understanding of the things of God?

Teamwork

Read Matthew 20:1-16. Apply the principles for interpreting parables to it. This can be done in smaller groups for greater interaction. Try to get at the central truth of the passage; then apply that truth to your life in specific ways.

Reaching the Summit

Encourage one another by reading Matthew 7:24-27, a parable Jesus used to commend those who understand and obey his teaching.

Next Session

Letters are powerful tools for communication. When we receive a personal letter from a distant friend or family member, it can light up a dismal day. If you feel comfortable, bring a letter you have received in the last six to twelve months (e-mails are acceptable but letters are preferred). Be prepared to read a portion of the letter that really impacted you.

Close in Prayer

Try to devote some of your prayer time to developing prayer partners. Pair up with someone for the next thirty days, agreeing to call one another between meetings and pray for each other.

Session 5

Unpacking an Epistle

Drawing truth from New Testament letters without compromising their intent.

Establishing Base Camp

Earlier this year I was visiting my family outside Tampa, Florida, and needed to find an important document belonging to my father. It was an urgent need and he was not home at the moment, so I took the liberty of searching for it. Opening the drawer where he kept such items—old war medals, awards from his coaching career, certificates recognizing degrees earned—I noticed a stack of cards and letters neatly bound in a rubber band. I immediately recognized them. My dad had kept every letter we'd written, every birthday card, Father's Day greeting and note to "Grandpa" from my kids. They were part of his lifelong treasure chest, available at any moment to read again and again. Each word or thought is eternally inscribed upon the paper and upon his heart.

I was deeply moved when I saw those letters. It showed me how much my father loved us, that he has a depth of soul that ponders things far more significant than the sports page or the latest political poll. I realize now how important those simple notes and cards are to him, and remember that whenever I write him, my words will once again become part of a loved and historic treasury.

✔ Take a moment to reflect upon a letter that you still keep or that you remember. Is it a love letter? wisdom from a seasoned mentor? an accolade from a colleague? a written "snapshot" of a family memory? Describe it and why you keep it.

Mapping the Trail

Letters are dangerous. They can evoke great passions that stir the imagination, or they can unearth heartbreaking emotions that cripple, shame and destroy the reader. A person must take pause before writing a letter, because the words have lasting impact and can be "resurrected" many times over to refresh the memory of the reader—for sorrow or for joy. In this way "the pen is mightier than the sword" because it wields great power, a power that can be unleashed for immeasurable good or intense harm. I tend to keep the letters I like and trash the others. A file in my office labeled "Day-makers" is loaded with notes, cards and letters of encouragement or gratitude that I reread from time to time.

The New Testament letters (the Epistles) are also filled with encouragement and gratitude. But they contain truth that confronts readers with their sin and lack of love for Christ and others. They weren't kept because the readers "liked" everything in them but because they were words of love, hope, rebuke and challenge from God. Churches relied on these letters for guidance for the Christian life in an oppressive and dangerous world.

✓ Is there a particular New Testament letter to which you turn for strength, hope or guidance? Explain why.

Beginning the Ascent

Increasingly in our culture, letter writing has fallen by the wayside, dying a slow death at the hands of an increasingly visual and verbal society. We continue the tradition of letter writing in the form of e-mail, but this does not qualify as true letter writing. In the days the Bible was written, letters were the only forms of permanent and historic communication. Though word of mouth was a trustworthy and essential communication tool for centuries, only letters and other written documents could capture the heart of a culture and give it a life beyond the years of its members. Writing materials were scarce, few people knew how to write and it took a long time to compose documents. Letters were treasured, especially those written by the apostles speaking under the inspiration of the Holy Spirit to the church. The New Testament Epistles fanned the flames of faith for Christ-followers and were copied and circulated from one church to another, eventually bound together in "books" for ready reference.

What is an epistle? In the New Testament, an epistle is a deeply passionate letter directed to a church or person for the purpose of instruction, edification and hope. Some Bible scholars have reduced them to simply a set of doctrinal propositions to be obeyed, but this misses the point. We must remember that these letters also reveal the heart of God and the soul of the writer. Filled with great emotion and zeal, the Epistles are lifegiving and capture the heart and mind of the readers so that the readers are pulled closer to Christ and his will for the church.

✓ What emotions do you find in Paul's first letter to the Corinthians, "I am not writing this to shame you, but to warn you, as my dear children" (1 Corinthians 4:14)?

✓ What is the tone of Paul's writing from a prison cell to the Philippians? "Finally, my brothers, rejoice in the Lord! It is no trouble for me to write the same things to you again, and it is a safeguard for you" (3:1).

The occasional nature of the Epistles. One of the reasons the Epistles can at times be difficult to interpret is that they were initially intended for a certain audience to address specific issues in given situations. This does not mean that they are void of general truths for all believers for all time. But we must be cautious in directly applying a specific truth in a general way. Read the following verses:

> I write these things to you who believe in the name of the Son of God so that you may know that you have eternal life. (1 John 5:13)

> Confident of your obedience, I write to you, knowing that you will do even more than I ask. (Philemon 1:21)

> Dear friends, although I was very eager to write to you about the salvation we share, I felt I had to write and urge you to contend for the faith that was once for all entrusted to the saints. (Jude 1:3)

✓ Which of these is intended for a general audience and which for a specific? Look at the context of each of these passages before you decide. Read a few verses before and after to get a feel for the statement.

How are Epistles structured? Each epistle is unique. Epistles don't follow a specific structure. They share some common elements, but there are also many variations. Nonetheless it will help to be aware of some basic elements.

The Structure of an Epistle
(Taken from *How to Read the Bible for All Its Worth* by Gordon Fee and Douglas Stuart, and the *Zondervan Pictorial Encyclopedia of the Bible*)
1. name of writer and recipient
2. personal greeting
3. prayers or thanksgiving for the spiritual or temporal welfare of the readers
4. main teaching (doctrinal discussion, instruction and application of truth)
5. benediction or final salutation

Not all epistles have all of the components listed above. For example, 1 John contains only the main teaching, and 2 Peter and James lack a final benediction. However, we can use the structure in most cases to understand the purpose of the letter, the audience, the perspective of the writer and the application to the church today.

Kinds of epistles. Scholars have used the following categories to group the Epistles:

☐ Pauline Epistles (thirteen letters from Paul)
1. Letters to churches

Romans	2 Corinthians
1 Corinthians	Galatians
Ephesians	1 Thessalonians
Philippians	2 Thessalonians
Colossians	

2. Letters to individuals

1 Timothy	Titus
2 Timothy	Philemon

☐ General Epistles (eight letters)

Hebrews	1 John
James	2 John
1 Peter	3 John
2 Peter	Jude

Sometimes 1 & 2 Timothy and Titus are referred to as the Pastoral Epistles because they are Paul's instructions to young church leaders. Application of the truths in them, however, must not be limited to pastors or leaders alone. As a matter of fact, neither Timothy nor Titus were *pastors* in the sense we use the word today. They were actually sent by Paul for a set period of time to put the church in order, not to remain as the official pastor. See 1 Timothy 5:17, where clearly plural leadership was the biblical approach, and Titus 3:12, where Titus's time in Crete is assumed to be limited.

How do we unpack the truth in an epistle for our day? Principles of interpretation for epistles have some elements in common with the general guidelines of sound interpretation. But there are some unique components that must be recognized as well. Here are some guidelines to use when seeking to understand and apply the Epistles.

Guidelines for Interpreting an Epistle

Step 1. Read through the epistle at least once without stopping. After all, it was intended as a letter and should be read as such.

Step 2. Understand the historical setting (or context). What do we know about the author, audience and culture? Remember, this is a letter to a specific group of people, and we want to know as much about them as possible so we can understand why the author is writing to them.

Step 3. Look for problems or issues that seem to be the focus of attention. Why is the author writing? What need is being addressed? This will help you understand the purpose for writing.

Step 4. Discern the truth being spoken to the original hearers. What specifically is the author saying to them? How much of this is uniquely for them?

Step 5. Determine which part or parts of that truth are equally applicable to you or your church. To what extent is this truth transferable to your setting?

Now we'll look at a couple passages and apply some of the steps to each of them.

✓ Read Romans 1:1-7, and see if you can discern the reason for writing the letter.

✓ What clues do you find about the author, recipients and focus of the letter? Consult the introduction to Romans in a study Bible for more information.

✓ Read 1 Corinthians 6:1-8, and look briefly for teaching that applies to us. How would this apply to two believers in church today?

✓ How would this passage apply to a believer who has had toxic waste dumped on his property and the corporation responsible refuses to clean it up or pay for it to be removed?

Gaining a Foothold

Fee and Stuart suggest two rules when interpreting New Testament writings. The first may not apply to every component of a prophetic vision, but it serves us very well in the New Testament Epistles.

Rule 1: A text cannot mean what it never could have meant to its original authors or hearers.

Rule 2: Whenever we share comparable particulars (such as, similar specific life situations) with the first-century setting, God's Word to us is the same as his Word to them.

Trailmarkers

One of the great verses for proper interpretation and application of God's Word is 2 Timothy 2:15. Although it was given to a specific person (Timothy), it has general application principles for all who study and teach the Bible. Another is Ezra 7:10, which emphasizes the importance of diligent study and putting the truth into practice *before* teaching others.

Find a partner and memorize 2 Timothy 2:15 or Ezra 7:10, working diligently to heed the truths in them.

Teamwork

We are going to do an exercise using Philippians. Paul primarily wrote to thank the Philippians for the gift they had sent him while he was detained in Rome. Philippi was a Roman colony, and its inhabitants were Roman citizens. They were proud to be Romans, even dressing like them and speaking Latin. Paul reminded the believers they had a better, heavenly citizenship (3:20-21). The letter is packed with the theme of joy despite Paul's imprisonment and exhorts believers to live a life worthy of the gospel. It contains warnings against legalists and grace abusers alike and calls people to follow Christ's example of humble service and love.

"If Christian truth and Christian living are brought together (as they are in the New Testament), and if the basis for both is thoroughly understood by sound theological interpretation in the Old and New Testament, a new power and a new unity will appear among Christians even though they are separated organizationally along denominational lines." (A. Berkeley Mickelsen, *Interpreting the Bible*)

✔ Open your Bibles to Philippians 4:1-13, and work in smaller teams to complete this exercise. Follow steps 3, 4 and 5 of "Guidelines for Interpreting an Epistle."

✓ What truths does Paul speak primarily to the Philippians?

✓ What principles apply to us as well?

✓ What problems is Paul facing personally that we can learn from, even though the text is not primarily addressing these problems?

Reaching the Summit

Applying biblical truth in meaningful and consistent ways is very important to every generation. Interpretation is challenging because we are so far removed from the original historical and cultural context. These guidelines should help clear some of the fog. For a more complete discussion on biblical interpretation, look at *Interpretation* in the Bible 101 series.

Take a few minutes to clear up any questions you have, and be encouraged by the progress you have made.

Next Session

Review the previous sessions. We will look at some Scripture that will help pull together all that we have learned about the various forms of Bible literature.

Close in Prayer

Pray that you will respond with diligence when it comes to studying the Bible. So often we look for a few verses to meet our immediate need and then misapply them. It's worth it to do the work of careful study (described in 2 Timothy 2:15) so that we obey those truths that are directed to us and avoid misinterpreting those that do not. Pray for one another in this regard.

Session 6

Putting It All Together

Bringing together the many types of literature we have been studying over the past five sessions to gain confidence in reading and interpreting them.

Establishing Base Camp

"Are you going to try the wall?"

The wall. That's what people at camp called it. There was something ominous about the way they described it.

"It's not really that bad," they said. Anything that has to be described in relationship to "bad" always turns out to be worse than people say.

I put a big, confident smile on my face so as not to scare my nine-year-old son, and we set out to climb *the wall*. With harnesses, carabiners, ropes and helmets we prepared ourselves at two separate faces of the wall. It was a fifty-five-foot-high wooden structure with three angled faces. Each face was about six feet wide and had a series of hand and footholds that looked like odd-shaped rocks ascending to the top. These little rocks were bolted to the wall and scattered two or three feet apart from one another. You climb with your own strength but are safe from falling because someone is holding the ropes that will break your fall as you rappel downward a few feet. I would lead the way as my son, Ryan, watched.

The first ten feet were great. Awkward, but not very frightening. Halfway up I looked down. Big mistake. Somehow thirty feet seems higher than when you are on the ground. I remember the sheer terror that came over me. My cognitive powers said: *You're fine, you can't fall. If you slip, you will hang securely in your harness until you get your footing back. No problem.* But then the emotional side of my brain spoke up: *You're nuts; if you fall, you will be an oil spot on the asphalt of life! People die after falling off six-foot ladders. How can you even think about going the next twenty-five feet to the top? Get down. You are forty. People will understand.*

Then another part of me spoke: *Your son and six others are watching, including an eight-year-old who climbed the wall in about thirty-five seconds just minutes ago. If you quit you will have a plaque with your name on it hung in the "Climbing Hall of Shame" in Wimptown, Ohio* (next to the Baseball Hall of Fame in Cooperstown). *Your son will be forever marked by fear and live the rest of his life in a commune.* Motivated by this third voice, I completed the ascent.

I was relieved to reach the top, until the guides said, "Okay, now let go of the handholds and just lean back." This is like saying to an airline passenger, "Just open the door and step out." This time, I refused to look down as I rappelled backward down the wall, firmly supported by the ropes connected to my harness. The earth never felt so good. Like a hostage held for months by international terrorists, I kissed the ground and thanked God for creating the force of gravity.

✓ Describe a time when someone or something intimidated you. Perhaps it was a boss, an opponent or a difficult task. How did you deal with it?

 Mapping the Trail

In this session we will look at some passages in the book of Hebrews. It is a New Testament book that relies heavily on the Old Testament for the message it communicates. In the book you will find all the literature we discussed except for a parable. Because of the numerous Old Testament quotes, you will find proverbs, prophecy and psalms in the epistle.

Hebrews is addressed to Jewish believers who may have been tempted to return to the sacrificial system of Judaism. The author, whose name is unknown, writes to challenge and encourage these believers. It has often been an intimidating book to many people because of the kinds of literature in it. Just like "the wall," it can look very difficult, but if you're willing to do the work, you will make great progress.

✓ What other books of the Bible are most intimidating for you to study? Describe why.

✓ Has doing this study helped you gain confidence in reading some of these books again? Why or why not?

Teamwork

Complete the exercises listed below, referring as necessary to the previous sessions for understanding psalms, proverbs and prophecy. Divide into groups of three to five to work on these questions.

✓ Based on Hebrews 1:1-4, what is the main theme of the book? What kind of literature is this passage?

✓ After you answer the questions above, look at the notes in a study Bible, and skim through the introduction to the book for some background material.

✓ Read Hebrews 2:5-9. Look up the cross-reference to the Old Testament passage quoted. What kind of literature is it? What kinds of parallelisms occur in verses 6-8? What point is the author making about Jesus?

✓ Jesus is shown as the supreme high priest of a new covenant, better than the old covenant made with Moses. In Hebrews 8 this comparison is detailed. Read chapter 8 through once. Then return to verses 7-13. What kind of literature is found in verses 8-12?

✓ Look up the original Old Testament passage and see what the context is. Who was the original audience? What is this passage about?

✓ Why do the author's words bring comfort to the Old Testament audience? How do the same words bring hope to the readers of Hebrews?

✓ Read Hebrews 9:11-15. What does this say about the Old Testament system as compared to Christ's work on the cross?

✓ The writer exhorts the believers to persevere and live holy lives in the midst of trial and difficulty. In 12:4-11 readers are challenged to be disciplined. Read the verses aloud together. Look up any Old Testament cross-references that might be listed for verses 5 and 6. What kind of literature is the writer using here?

✓ Why is this kind of literature especially helpful to quote?

✓ How are these words an encouragement to the readers?

Reaching the Summit

The book of Hebrews integrates many unique forms of literature. Celebrate some of the insights you received now that you have some skills to read this Scripture profitably. Read Hebrews 10:24-25, and consider memorizing those verses.

Next Session

Discuss what to study next. You might plan a special event that will allow you to have fun and build some deeper relationships before you start your next series.

Close in Prayer

Read Hebrews 12:28-29, and use it as a reference point for your prayer time. Pray for group needs and concerns as well.

Leader's Notes

Few ventures are more defining than leading a group that produces changed lives and sharper minds for the cause of Christ. At Willow Creek we have seen small groups transform our church, offer deeper levels of biblical community and provide an environment where truth can be understood and discussed with enthusiasm. So we have focused on a group-based study rather than a classroom-lecture format or individual study (though these studies can profitably be used in both settings with minor adaptations).

Each method of learning has its strengths; each has its weaknesses. In personal study one can spend as little or as much time as desired on an issue and can focus specifically on personal needs and goals. The downside: there is no accountability to others, no one to challenge thoughts or assumptions, no one to provide support when life comes tumbling down around you. The classroom is ideal for proclaiming truth to many at one time and for having questions answered by those with expertise or knowledge in a subject area. But the pace of the class depends largely on the teacher, and there is limited time to engage in the discussion of personal issues. The small group is optimal for life-on-life encouragement, prayer and challenge. And it provides a place where learning is enhanced through the disciplines of biblical community. But small groups are usually not taught by content experts and cannot focus solely on one person's needs.

Our hope is that you will be able to use this curriculum in a way that draws from the best of all three methods. Using the small group as a central gathering place, personal preparation and study will allow you to focus on your own learning and growth goals. The small group activity will provide you with an engaging environment for refining your understanding and gaining perspective into the lives and needs of others. And perhaps by inviting a knowledgeable outsider to the group (or a cluster of small groups at a Saturday seminar, for example) you could gain the benefits of solid teaching in a given subject area. In any case your devotion to Christ, your commitment to your local church and your obedience to the Word of God are of utmost importance to us. Our desire is to see you "grow in the grace and knowledge of the Lord Jesus Christ."

Leadership Tips

Here are some basic guidelines for leaders. For more extensive leadership support and training we recommend that you consult *The Willow Creek Guide to Leading Lifechanging Small Groups,* where you will find many suggestions for leading creative groups.

Using the leader's notes. The questions in the study will not be repeated in the leader's notes. Instead, we have provided comments, clarifications, additional information, leadership tips or group exercises. These will help you guide the discussion and keep the meeting on track.

Shared leadership. When leading a small group remember that your role is to guide the discussion and help draw people into the group process. Don't try to be the expert for everything. Seek to involve others in the leadership process and activities of group life (hosting meetings, leading prayer, serving one another, leading parts of the discussion and so forth).

Preparation. Your work between meetings will determine group effectiveness during meetings. Faithful preparation does not mean that you will control the meeting or that it will move exactly as you planned. Rather, it provides you with a guiding sense of the desired outcomes of the time together so that you can gauge the pace of the meeting and make adjustments along the way. Above all, make sure you are clear about the overall goal of the meeting. Then, even if you get appropriately sidetracked dealing with a personal concern or a discussion of related issues, you can graciously help the group refocus on the goal of the meeting. Also, preparation will allow you to observe how others are engaging with the material. *You should complete the study* before coming to the meeting. You can participate in the group activities at the meeting, but take time to become personally acquainted with the material in case you need to alter the schedule or amount of time on each section.

Purpose. The series is designed to help people understand the Word and be confident in their ability to read, study and live its lifechanging truths. Bible 101 is not designed for a group whose primary goal is caregiving or support. That does not mean you will avoid caring for each other, praying for needs or supporting one another through personal crises. It simply means that the *entire* focus of the group is not for these purposes. At the same time, the content should never take precedence over the process of transformation. There will be appropriate times to set the curriculum aside and pray. Or you may want to spend an evening having fun together. Remember, Jesus did not say, "Go therefore into all the world and complete the curriculum." Our focus is to make disciples. The curriculum is a tool, not a master. Use it consistently and with discernment, and your group will be well-served. But be clear about the primary focus of the group as you gather, and remind people every few weeks about the core purpose so that the group does not drift. So even though this is designed for six meetings per study guide, you might take longer if you have a meeting that focuses entirely on prayer or service.

Length of Meeting. We assume that you have about seventy to ninety minutes for this meeting, including prayer and some social time. If you have more or less time, adjust accordingly, especially if you have a task-based group. In that case, since you must complete the task (working on a ministry team or serving your church in some way), you will have to be selective in what you cover unless you can devote at least one hour to the meeting. In the format described below, feel free to play with the time allowed for "Beginning the Ascent," "Trailmarkers" and "Teamwork." We have given general guidelines for time to spend on each section. But depending on the size of group (we recommend about eight members), familiarity with the Bible and other group dynamics, you will have to make adjustments. After a few meetings you should have a good idea of what it will take to accomplish your goals.

Format. We have provided you with a general format. But feel free to provide some creativity or a fresh approach. You can begin with prayer, for example, or skip the "Establishing Base Camp" group opener and dive right into the study. We recommend that you follow the format closely early in the group process. As your group and your leadership skills mature and progress, you should feel increasing freedom to bring your creativity and experience to the meeting format. Here is the framework for the format in each of the guides in this series.

 Establishing Base Camp

This orients people to the theme of the meeting and usually involves a group opener or icebreaker. Though not always directly related to the content, it will move people toward the direction for the session. A base camp is the starting point for any mountain journey.

 Mapping the Trail

In this component we get clear about where we will go during the meeting. It provides an overview without giving away too much and removing curiosity.

 Beginning the Ascent

This is the main portion of the meeting: the climb toward the goal. It is the teaching and discussion portion of the meeting. Here you will find questions and explanatory notes. You will usually find the following two components included.

Pullouts. These provide additional detail, clarification or insight into content or questions that may arise in the participants' minds during the session.

Charts/Maps. Visual learners need more than words on a page. Charts, maps and other visuals combined with the content provide a brief, concise summary of the information and how it relates.

Gaining a Foothold

Along the trail people can drift off course or slip up in their understanding. These footholds are provided for bringing them into focus on core issues and content.

 Trailmarkers

These are key biblical passages or concepts that guide our journey. Participants will be encouraged to memorize or reflect on them for personal growth and for the central biblical basis behind the teaching.

 Teamwork

This is a group project, task or activity that builds a sense of community and shared understanding. It will be different for each study guide and for each lesson, depending on the author's design and the purpose of the content covered.

 Reaching the Summit

This is the end of the content discussion, allowing members to look back on what they have learned and capture it in a brief statement or idea. This "view from the top" will help them once again focus on the big picture after spending some time on the details.

Balancing caregiving and study/discussion. One of the most difficult things to do in a group, as I alluded to above, is balancing the tension between providing pastoral and mutual care to members and getting through the material. I have been in small groups where needs were ignored to get the work done, and I have been in groups where personal needs were the driving force of the group to the degree that the truth of the Word was rarely discussed. These guides are unique because they are designed to train and teach processes that must take place in order to achieve its purpose. But the group would fail miserably if someone came to a meeting and said, "I was laid off today from my job," and the group said a two-minute prayer and then opened their curriculum. So what do you do? Here are some guidelines.

1. People are the most important component of the group. They have real needs. Communicate your love and concern for people, even if they don't always get all the work done or get sidetracked.

2. When people disclose hurts or problems, address each disclosure with empathy and prayer. If you think more time should be devoted to someone, set aside time at the end of the meeting, inviting members to stay for additional prayer or to console the person. Cut the meeting short by ten minutes to accomplish this. Or deal with it right away for ten to fifteen minutes, take a short break, then head into the study.

3. Follow up with people. Even if you can't devote large portions of the meeting time to caregiving, you and others from the group can provide this between meetings over the phone or in other settings. Also learn to leverage your time. For example, if your meeting begins at 7:00 p.m., ask the member in need and perhaps one or two others from the group to come at 6:30 p.m. for sharing and prayer. A person will feel loved, your group will share in the caregiving, and it is not another evening out for people.

4. Assign prayer partners or groups of three to be little communities within the group. Over the phone or on occasional meetings outside the group (before church and so on) they could connect and check in on how life is going.

5. For serious situations solicit help from others, including pastors or other staff at church. Do not go it alone. Set boundaries for people with serious care needs, letting them know that the group can devote some but not substantial meeting time to support them. "We all know that Dave is burdened by his son's recent illness, so I'd like to spend the first ten minutes tonight to lift him up in prayer and commit to support Dave through this season. Then, after our meeting I'd like us to discuss any specific needs you (Dave) might have over the next two to three weeks (such as meals, help with house chores, etc.) and do what we can to help you meet those needs." Something to that effect can keep the group on track but still provide a place to express compassion.

Take time to look at the entire series if you have chosen only one of the guides. Though each can be used as a stand-alone study, there is much to benefit from in the other guides because each covers material essential for a complete overview of how to study and understand the Bible. We designed the guides in series form so that you can complete them in about a year if you meet weekly, even if you take a week off after finishing each guide.

A Word About Leadership

One of your key functions as a small group leader is to be a cheerleader—someone who seeks out signs of spiritual progress in others and makes some noise about it. What have you seen God doing in your group members' lives as a result of this study? Don't assume they've seen that progress—and definitely don't assume they are beyond needing simple words of encouragement. Find ways to point out to people the growth you've seen. Let them know it's happening, and that it's noticeable to you and others.

There aren't a whole lot of places in this world where people's spiritual progress is going to be recognized and celebrated. After all, wouldn't you like to hear someone say somthing like that to you? Your group members feel the same way. You have the power to make a profound impact through a sincere, insightful remark.

Be aware also that some groups get sidetracked by a difficult member or situation that hasn't been confronted. And some individuals could be making significant progress, but they just need a nudge. "Encouragement" is not about just saying "nice" things; it's about offering *words that urge*. It's about giving courage (en*courage*-ment) to those who lack it.

So leaders, take a risk. Say what needs to be said to encourage your members as they grow in their knowledge of the Bible. Help them not just amass more information, but move toward the goal of becoming fully devoted followers of Jesus Christ. Go ahead; make their day!

Session 1. Experiencing a Psalm.

Introduce the Session (1 min.) Go over the purpose and goal.

Purpose: To help people understand the rich nature of Hebrew poetry as expressed in the Psalms and to gain skills for understanding the meaning of a given psalm.

Goal: To equip each group member to understand the structure and kinds of psalms so they can be interpreted and applied appropriately to life.

Establishing Base Camp (10 min.) This opening section is designed to give people a glimpse of what biblical poetry is all about. We will chip away at some of the stereotypes concerning poetry, and discover what ideas people already have about poetry. A few still may find poetry simple or childish. Remind them that one of the greatest poets in history killed a giant with a slingshot when he was still a young teen.

Mapping the Trail (10 min.) Parallelisms function to give the Psalms their structure and meaning. Review these with the group because it forms the basis for interpreting the text. Reinforce the fact that we are not in the labeling business. We simply want to raise an awareness of how this literature functions in the Bible. Read the Leland Ryken quote in the pullout to highlight this point.

Beginning the Ascent (30 min.) The Psalms are filled with the heartfelt expressions of real people facing real life. Much of our culture still clings to guarded relationships and well-postured images designed to hide our true selves. But the Psalms pull no punches in this regard. The realism and passion of these songs, many written for worship services, probe the depths of the heart of each person who is open to experience them.

The discussion question here is aimed at uncovering our fears or at least breaking our worship paradigm, which may represent the Christian as a composed, steady and controlled personality. Order in worship is important, but within that order is the freedom to speak our heart. We are fearful because we're not sure what others will think of us, or our reputation will be damaged or we may no longer be viewed as "having it all together."

Push a little here to show your group that God wants us to worship with heart, soul, mind and strength. And that means unleashing some of our great needs, feelings, disappointments and dreams in his presence. Encourage members to find psalms that match their feelings and read them to God.

Images are often created with metaphors and similes. Emphasize the use of figurative language used in poetry to make the truth more vivid and memorable. Many people think in pictures, and the Psalms are great places for creating images that can be remembered.

Review the types of psalms with the group so that they will appreciate the robust mixture of hymns and songs and how they were used in worship.

Gaining a Foothold (3 min.) Read this to your group.

Trailmarkers (10 min.) Psalm 1 is a very popular psalm and worth memorizing. Some will rise to the challenge, while others may simply prefer to meditate on it—which is encouraged in the psalm! Use your judgment as to whether you should ask members to memorize or meditate. Perhaps some mediation and debriefing would be good now, and you could make a commitment to memorize at least verses 1-3 before the next meeting.

Teamwork (15 min.) Complete this as a group. We are staying with Psalm 1 because it will really drive Hebrew parallelism home to them, and it's also a very good yet brief passage for our purposes.

Verse	Parallelism
1	Synonymous
2	Synthetic
3	Climactic (it builds on each line)
4	Synthetic
5	Synonymous
6	Antithetic

This is a wisdom psalm, reading in some ways like a proverb, contrasting the consequences of right versus wrong living. The words *fruit, water* and *tree,* and the use of *standing* and *sitting* are all ways that figures of speech create images to drive home the truth. A phrase like *day and night* in Hebrew—used also in Joshua 1:8—simply means regularly and consistently (not that the righteous do not sleep!). All of these combine to make this a powerful and memorable psalm. It is both understood and experienced because the reader can feel the emotion and identify with the word pictures.

Reaching the Summit (5 min.) Take a moment to get any final feedback or deal with any lingering questions. For those who want to complete further study, encourage them to read the entry for "Psalms" in a Bible dictionary (like the *New Bible Dictionary*) or a Bible encyclopedia.

Next Session (5 min.) We will continue with another form of Hebrew poetry—the proverb. These are often misunderstood or misapplied. Proverbs 1:1-7 lays the foundation for the study, so ask members to read that brief Scripture and make the list as described.

Close in Prayer (10 min.) You might select a group member to read a portion of a psalm as part of your prayer time. Look at Psalm 5 or Psalm 8 as possibilities.

Session 2. Applying a Proverb.
Introduce the Session (3 min.) Go over the purpose and goal.

Purpose: To help group members avoid the common mistakes made when reading and applying proverbs to their lives.

Goal: To provide members with the tools they need to properly interpret a proverb in its context and apply it meaningfully and accurately to a life situation.

Establishing Base Camp (10 min.) Wisdom comes to us from many sources, but our goal is to focus on biblical wisdom, particularly as found in Proverbs. Use this question to discover what people look for in a wise person. Usually, experience and a proven track record are at the top of the list. Begin to focus on why wisdom from others is important in life.

Mapping the Trail (10 min.) The purpose of biblical wisdom is to provide skill for living life. Some benefits listed in Proverbs 1:1-7 include the ability to
* make sound judgments.
* do what is just and fair in God's eyes
* help younger men and women gain knowledge and understanding
* make the wise even wiser in their discernment
* understand proverbs and parables, whose meanings are often obscure to the unlearned or foolish

• understand that all true wisdom comes from God

Beginning the Ascent (30 min.) Make sure that members can see the parallels that exist between wisdom from the Scripture and from the world. In some ways they are the same. Wise sayings are not intended to be applied in every setting. A look at these common words of wisdom helps them see this before we go into the biblical text with great detail.

1. Not everyone who is early will become wealthy or avoid all sickness, but the point of this saying is to encourage diligence.

2. Sometimes it pays not to look. In an emergency situation you may have to leap away from an oncoming car. If you take time to look for the right place to jump, you may become a bumper sticker.

3. Not really. This saying obviously was popular before the income tax was invented. In most cases we need to earn at least $1.30 in order to save a buck!

4. When facing a pit bull, I will trade in the pen for a sword in a microsecond!

In going over the guidelines for interpreting proverbs, take your time to review the examples with the group. Give them time to ask questions and make clarifications. Remember the key is that this is a special kind of literature that most Westerners are less familiar with. We tend to be people of statement and fact, of data and logic. Proverbs don't always follow those rules but are nonetheless means of conveying truth.

Gaining a Foothold (5 min.) Review these with the group. It will be a ready reference for an exercise in the "Teamwork" section.

Trailmarkers (10 min.) These are important verses, particularly Proverbs 1:7, which is really the key verse of the entire book. At least take time to reflect on it or to memorize it.

Teamwork (15 min.) Proverbs 24:30-34 is one of my favorite passages. It depicts the value of work and the consequences of sloth so well. Here are some replies to the questions.

1. What images are being created by the writer? Sleep and slumber here are metaphors for laziness. The image of poverty coming like a bandit or armed robber creates a sudden terror. Even the actual description of the property makes it easy to envision.

2. Look at session one for a review if you need it. Verse 30 = synonymous, verse 31 = climactic, verse 32 = synonymous, verse 33 = climactic, and verse 34 = synonymous.

3. How does the writer use exaggeration (hyperbole) to make his point? The phrases "thorns had come up *everywhere*" and "the ground was *covered* with weeds" are there to imply the extent to which the neglect had taken place. It isn't intended to mean that there wasn't a square inch of property without a thorn on it or a patch of earth that had no weed on it.

4. What is being emphasized here? What is the wisdom principle?

What appears to us to be a gradual decline in diligence will one day lead to a great calamity. Poverty doesn't come in an instant to this man. He started with an extra few minutes away from the task he was supposed to do—the minutes became hours, then days. Now the result is catastrophic.

Notice in verse 33 how the writer starts with the most intense mode of laziness (sleep) and ends with folding his hands. We all know that too much sleep—the kind that takes the place of diligent, responsible work—will lead to loss of job, income and more. But the writer traces it back to the root cause. It all started with an extra nap here and there.

5. What is not being emphasized? (For example, is sleep bad?)

Here is where the workaholic will seek justification for his overwork. But the proverb doesn't suggest or allow this. The focus is the development of a lazy habit that grows like a thorn bush, eventually choking out the life of the nearby plant. Sleep and rest are not the focus—laziness and neglect are the problems.

It also isn't teaching that everyone who has property that is in disrepair is lazy and not working hard. Stick to the focus and the context, and learn the wisdom principle.

Reaching the Summit (5 min.) Allow time for any final questions or comments here. Review any material you think needs another quick overview or reminder. Affirm the group for working hard and remind them of the benefits of understanding the wisdom of Proverbs.

Next Session (10 min.) Ask a member or two to come to the next meeting and describe a prophecy they have heard or read. Did it come true? What is their response to this? Most people think "prophecy" is about predicting the future, so they will expect you to speak in terms of prediction and fulfillment. It is a good setup for next session when we will show that there is much more to prophecy than predicting future events.

Closing Prayer (10 min.) As a reminder of the last session, encourage someone to read a psalm as a prayer. The psalms often express people's greatest fears and hopes and are very applicable to our daily lives. You might have a few options ready in addition to what is suggested here. Continue to minister to group needs as well.

Session 3. Deciphering a Prophecy.
Introduce the Session (3 min.) Go over the purpose and goal.

Purpose: To help members remove some of the doubt and fear of reading prophetic literature and see the role it plays in bringing God's message to us.

Goal: To be able to read a prophecy and gain insight into its teaching and application to the historical setting and today's world.

 Establishing Base Camp (10 min.) Much prophecy uses images and word pictures. We want people to understand that this is a normal means of communication, especially in today's visual culture. Help the group reflect on the power of images to convey truth or solidify a memory. Use this discussion to get to know each other better as life stories unfold in response to the question.

Mapping the Trail (10 min.) Prophecy conferences that began in the 1920s and 30s and peaked in the 70s were helpful but often placed undue emphasis on the predictive nature of prophecy. Much prophecy is exhortation, a call to conform again to the law and truth of God. But most people think of prophecy primarily in terms of predicting the future, elaborate dating schemes, bizarre imagery often mistaken for literal pictures of the future kingdom, and so on. Television prophecy gurus are constantly linking current events to such schemes and yet are rarely held accountable when they are wrong.

The role of prophecy was never to lay out chronological details of every event in the future, or God would have described them that way in Scripture, making it clear for all readers to grasp. True, some symbolic language is used, but the original audience was far less baffled by such symbols because the images were linked to historical realities they understood. We are so far removed from these historical and cultural realities that we are left only with the symbols and visions. Therefore it requires much more work and research for us to understand prophecy the way that the original audience did.

Beginning the Ascent (30 min.) Here we want members to understand that prophecy has a simple focal point: speaking God's words to people. In that sense, much preaching has a prophetic tone as God's truths are revealed and God's people are called to follow him with full devotion.

Prophets were primarily sent to correct Israel. In the Old Testament, prophets spoke authoritative words of God that were not to be debated. The phrase "Thus says the Lord" was used to convey this. In the New Testament prophecy takes on a more edifying and encouraging function to the church, exhorting us to obedience and building up the body. Keep the discussion focused here on the function of a prophet.

To prevent false prophets from leading God's people astray—something Peter warned the church of (2 Peter 2:1)—tests were given to prove a prophet's authenticity. In the Old Testament, because they did not have all of God's revelation written down as we do today, people relied on prophets for guidance and truth. God harshly judged those who claimed to speak for him but were not called by him to do so.

New Testament prophecy was subject to evaluation by the church, a safeguard to ensure that people did not misrepresent God's will for a given congregation. But they were not put to death for being wrong. The nature of New Testament prophecy was not the same as the office and role of the Old Testament prophet who was called to speak God's divine revelation to the people.

When you come to the section titled "Prophecy as Literature," walk people through the three types of prophecy and read the quote in the margin on visionary prophecy.

Ezekiel 34:1-10 is a strong rebuke to the leaders of Israel for neglecting the people.

Many may wonder about the gift of prophecy today. It is clear from 1 Corinthians 12—14 that this gift is alive and well but usually takes the form of exhortation and is subject to the discernment and wisdom of the church and the Word of God. It is to be used for edifying (not confusing, startling or impressing) the body of Christ and is to be expressed in orderly ways. There is no biblical ground for believers giving individual "prophetic words" to one another in flippant, haphazard or unevaluated settings.

As a group, review the ground rules and potential pitfalls in interpreting prophecy. It is a lot of material, and no one is expected to remember all this when reading the Bible. Encourage the group to keep this handy or write these guidelines inside the cover of their Bibles for future reference. It should help people read prophecy with more confidence.

It's important to tell the group that one session on how to interpret prophecy is insufficient to give them full confidence and skill for interpreting every prophetic passage of Scripture. This is a starting place. More study is required.

Gaining a Foothold (5 min.) Read this to your group and highlight the three approaches to prophetic interpretation. Most conservative Bible scholars adopt the second or third methods. The first method tends to deny the truthfulness of Scripture. Because there are different approaches to interpreting prophecy, make sure no one is criticized for adopting a certain method. The key is to determine what God is saying and then obey!

Trailmarkers (10 min.) These verses will help keep the group grounded in the true nature and purpose of prophecy. Prophecy is God-initiated and the interpretation of any prophetic teaching is subject to the church and the others who have prophetic gifts and discernment.

Teamwork (20 min.) This may seem like a lengthy passage, but it is divided into five sections of three verses each so that major themes can be emphasized. You may want to divide into smaller groups and assign sections if you think time will become an obstacle to completing this. Allow for ten minutes in the subgroups and a 5-10 minute debriefing as a larger group.

What kind of prophecy is this? This is a predictive prophecy about Jesus Christ.

What figures of speech are used? There are many; here are most of them:

• Kings will "shut their mouths" means that they will be astonished at how he suffers and then is exalted.

• The "arm of the Lord" reflects God's power.

• He will grow up a "tender shoot" and a "root" means that he is a man of humble beginnings.

• That he will be "pierced" and "crushed" for us has some literal fulfillment (Christ was indeed pierced with nails and a spear) but also is a figure for suffering.

- We are "like sheep" who have left our master and wandered astray.
- He was like a "lamb" led to slaughter, innocent and submissive in his death.
- That he will "see his offspring" refers to his spiritual descendants because we know Christ did not marry.
- He will "divide the spoils" is a picture of a military victory, where the conqueror shares the rewards of the battle. Christ allows us to share in the kingdom with him.

How much of the prophecy is fulfilled? It is all fulfilled in Christ's coming and in his death on our behalf. This is a passage commonly referred to as the "gospel in the Old Testament."

What might apply to Israel here, and what applies to us? Israel probably understood this passage as a promise for deliverance by this servant and looked forward to his coming, but they did not have the cross to look back on as we do. So they probably did not see it as clearly as we can in light of Christ's life. Those hearing it in the seventh century B.C. would have found hope and comfort knowing that the messianic king would come. Jews later in history, following the teaching of many rabbis, see the servant as Israel the nation because they cannot understand why a messiah-king would allow himself to be killed. It is easier for them to see Israel as a nation suffering at the hands of oppressive governments and powerful nations.

We of course gain insight into the Christ, understanding that he "had nothing in his appearance that we should desire him." The Jesus portrayed by Hollywood movies often does not fit this description. He was despised, a "man of sorrows" and like one from whom "men hide their faces." We see the cross, the mistreatment of Christ and the willing sacrifice he made in obedience to his Father's will. And we also become more confident in the Word of God, which predicted all this almost seven hundred years before the cross. Finally we see the ultimate victory in which we share all things with Christ as promised in the New Testament.

This is the most quoted Old Testament passage in the New Testament. A study Bible will reveal New Testament cross-references for almost every stanza.

What do you learn about God and his work from this passage? He is sovereign, his timing is perfect, his will unstoppable, his plan fulfilled with grace. We see his love in allowing Christ to suffer and die for us, and we see his love for Jesus in that he exalted him above all others (Philippians 2)

Next Session (3 min.) Ask the group to read Matthew 13:11-16. This is placed right between the parable of the Sower and Jesus' explanation of what the parable means. Reading this before the next meeting will allow members to get a grasp on the mysterious nature of a parable and why Jesus chose to use them in his teaching.

Closing Prayer (10 min.) Encourage group members to reflect on our historical "roots" as believers in Christ. We have a church today that is built on the teaching of the prophets and the apostles, people God chose to reveal himself through. Also thank God for leaders in today's churches, especially yours, because they are responsible in the eyes of God for our spiritual well-being (Hebrews 13:17).

Session 4. Understanding a Parable.
Introduce the Session (3 min.) Go over the purpose and goal.

Purpose: To help people understand the use of parables in Jesus teaching.

Goal: To equip each member to read a parable and extract the central truth being communicated, applying that truth to our lives.

△ Establishing Base Camp (10 min.) Stories always capture our imagination. Help members see how stories leave an indelible impression on us and therefore are great for teaching truth in a memorable way. Though not every parable is a story, many are. Give people enough time to tell stories from their lives. This is a great way to get to know each other better and to set up the teaching for the session.

⊠ Mapping the Trail (10 min.) Some may wonder why it looks like God is hardening hearts so that people will not be able to understand his truth and enter the kingdom, even if they wanted to. A careful reading of the passage, and an understanding that God desires that no one should perish (2 Peter 3:9), reveals that people harden their hearts to God. In doing so they block out their future ability to hear the truth.

👟 Beginning the Ascent (30 min.) Help your group understand the basic idea of comparison in parabolic teaching. Jesus compared spiritual realities to physical ones in stories to help people understand his word. Don't let people get sidetracked with the details, assigning spiritual meanings to them.

Review the guidelines for interpreting a parable. These are fairly clear. We are not trying to memorize all these steps. Instead, use this as a framework when dealing with parables.

When you come to Matthew 21:28-32, simply allow someone to read the text aloud. Don't take a lot of time on the details. Listen carefully as it is read and identify the core truth that is highlighted.

Gaining a Foothold (3 min.) These additional pointers are also listed for insight and consideration as you study parables. Read through them together, and discuss any questions about them.

🖈 Trailmarkers (10 min.) Spiritually immature or hardened people do not easily understand parables. The verse in 1 Corinthians reinforces this. Spiritual discernment is important to the church because we deal primarily with spiritual matters, and we are engaged in a spiritual battle (Ephesians 6:12).

🖐 Teamwork (15 min.) This parable is fairly straightforward. Ask someone to read it through so that you hear it as Jesus told it. The primary focus is God's grace and his gracious gifts. We do not deserve what he gives us (salvation, forgiveness, spiritual gifts, blessings) just as the later workers did not deserve what they received. The others are jealous but have no reason to be. The owner fulfilled his agreement with them.

Be careful here to follow the guidelines. There is a central truth—grace. Do not let the group get sidetracked by reading hidden meanings into the details (for example, the foreman is an angel, the eleventh hour is the judgment day, the denarius is our salvation, the vineyard is the church and so on). Such identifications are not warranted by the story.

Note also that this is partly a response to Peter's question in 19:27. Peter wants to know what he earns for giving up so much to follow Christ. Jesus assures him that sacrifice yields rewards. But the parable also indicates that God gives out gifts as he pleases, not based on what we believe we have earned.

Reaching the Summit (5 min.) Reading Matthew 7:24-27 will encourage the group in their efforts to understand the teachings of Jesus through parables. It too is a parable. Remind them of the progress they have made so far and celebrate that.

Next Session (1 min.) Ask members to bring a letter. We will be looking at the New Testament letters to churches and individuals, and discovering how to unpack the teachings found in them.

Close in Prayer (10 min.) Jesus revealed his truth to build us up. Thank him for showing you the great mysteries of the kingdom. Pray for people not yet in the kingdom and ask God to give you opportunities to discuss spiritual matters with them, leading them to a conversation about Christ.

Session 5. Unpacking an Epistle.
Introduce the Session (3 min.) Go over the purpose and goal.

Purpose: To understand how a New Testament letter is structured and interpreted.

Goal: To discern what truths in an epistle are meant for the specific audience (church or person) that is addressed and which truths are applicable to us today as well.

Establishing Base Camp (10 min.) The question here is designed to get at the emotion behind the letters as well as the content of them. So often we view the New Testament Epistles as instruction manuals for right living and sound church government. Certainly the letters contain these elements. But we also want the group to see that these are letters from a person writing for God with a sense of urgency, passion and mission.

Try to draw out the "why" in this question, helping people see how letters move our hearts and touch our souls.

Mapping the Trail (10 min.) We all have favorite passages or New Testament books. I have always loved Ephesians for the sense of security I have in Christ (chapters 1-3) and community I share in the body (chapters 4-6). Others love Romans because it lays out the power, depth and breadth of the gospel (chapters 1-11) and practical guidelines for living out that gospel (chapters 12-16). For some it is the Spirit-filled walk of Galatians or the love of God expressed in 1 John. Again, focus on why this is important and try to connect the comments of group members with one another, showing what they have in common. Use this question not only to understand individuals but also to build community.

Beginning the Ascent (30 min.) *What is an epistle?* It is important to note that these letters are emotional as well as doctrinal. Ask members to express what they feel when they read the passages listed. You might turn to the text and read a few verses surrounding those listed, getting a feel for the circumstances and passion of the writer.

The occasional nature of the Epistles. Emphasize that though there is much in the Epistles that applies to us, there are also some specific issues relevant only to the audience addressed. Each letter had an occasion or purpose, often a response to a question or issue (see 1 Corinthians 7:1).

1 John 5:13: This is clearly applicable to all believers and written in such a way as to appeal to all audiences.

Philemon 1:21: The context here is very specific, but we can draw principles from how Philemon is exhorted by Paul to treat the runaway slave Onesimus. Don't allow this verse to sidetrack the group into a doctrinal discussion of how we all ought to give money to reimburse slaveowners for losses or how to prepare rooms for traveling missionaries!

Jude 1:3: Although this was written to a persecuted church threatened with false teachers, contending for the gospel will be a challenge to every church in every age. That challenge might look different than what is described here, and it may vary in intensity. But definitely there are principles that apply to us as well as to the first-century church.

How are epistles structured? This is not to be viewed as a rigid framework. But it does provide some guidelines. Formal letter-writing in the first century followed a pattern. Ours does too. Business letters, legal documents, wills and acceptance (or rejection) letters for college admission follow a set design for familiarity and convention.

Kinds of epistles. This information is here simply to give people an overview of how the books are designated. It is not intended for memorization. You might mention (for chronological purposes) that most of the letters (except for the Pastoral Epistles, Hebrews, the epistles of John and Jude) were written during the period of time covered by the book of Acts, including Paul's two-year imprisonment described in Acts 28:30.

How do we unpack the truth in an epistle for our day? These guidelines are fairly straightforward. Here's a little help regarding the questions about Romans 1:1-7: a study Bible should reveal that Paul's major theme was the gospel, and his audience was Gentiles. Paul reveals his standing (a servant), his calling (an apostle) and his mission (the propagation of the gospel.) The letter is designed to unpack the great power of the gospel to save the sinner and sanctify the believer until Christ comes. Help the group to see that understanding this context will aid in the interpretation of the letter. Paul's major focus of the gospel is the driving force behind his mission, and Rome is the seedbed for everything the gospel confronts—human power, self-promotion, idolatry, greed, sexual impurity and legalism.

The questions regarding 1 Corinthians 6:1-8 are designed to separate the general from the specific application in the epistle. For believers today, the principle is the same. Using rule 2 in "Gaining a Foothold," we see that we have enough particulars in common: we are believers, we are in a church, and we will have disagreements in personal business life that might normally lead to lawsuits. But we are not to treat one another this way.

But in the second case, regarding the corporation the Bible makes no reference in this verse on how to handle such a matter. No such things as "corporations" existed in the ancient Eastern world. In the case of a corporation owned by thousands of stockholders, legal recourse may be the only means of establishing and insuring justice. This passage does not prohibit entering into a justifiable lawsuit with a corporation, even one where believers may be working. The transferable principle is to seek a settlement and reconciliation outside the courts. But legal recourse is sometimes necessary and not forbidden, especially to promote justice, which is the primary role of government (Romans 13:1-7).

Gaining a Foothold (5 min.) Read this to the group and answer any questions about these rules. Basically we do not assign meaning to a text that it never could have had. The degree to which we can apply a text that was directed at a specific group of people will be proportional to the degree to which our circumstances and setting are similar. So, if we are in prison and long for a visit from a dear friend and coworker, we can identify with Paul's longing for Timothy to come to him and draw some comfort from Paul's patience and strength.

Trailmarkers (10 min.) Break into teams and memorize these verses together. Whatever you can't complete, finish before next session.

Teamwork (15 min.) The truths that are primarily for the Philippians are found in verse 2 (dissension between two members in the church), verse 3 (encouragement for fellow workers) and verse 10 (concern for Paul and his financial needs). The principles that apply to us as well are found in verses 4-9, which are relevant to us regardless of circumstances.

What problems is Paul facing personally that we can learn from, even though the text is not specifically addressing these problems? In verse 1 Paul is longing for contact with his friends, yet he rejoices and finds hope in writing them to encourage and thank them. In verses 11-12 Paul has learned to be content when he has abundant ministry and personal resources and also when he is lacking in them. We can learn to be content in our circumstances as well.

Reaching the Summit (5 min.) Take a few moments to encourage the group and handle final questions. Remind them that much of the New Testament consists of letters to individuals and churches, so it is valuable to understand the nature and interpretation of epistles.

Next Session (1 min.) We will look at a passage that requires the group to bring together all that they have learned. Encourage them to review the teaching on prophecy and poetry in preparation for this.

Close in Prayer (10 min.) Encourage the group for all they have learned, and pray for wisdom and discernment in seeking the truth from the Word.

Session 6. Putting It All Together.
Introduce the Session (3 min.) Go over the purpose and goal.

Purpose: To show how all that we have studied can give us confidence when we are reading some of the more challenging passages of the Bible.

Goal: To help members study the book of Hebrews by recognizing how the various types of literature are used to convey truth and encourage believers.

Establishing Base Camp (10 min.) Obstacles and fears can intimidate us all. Read this story and answer the questions at the end. We want people to know that it is normal to feel a sense of intimidation at times. Use this to prepare the group for the work ahead in the session.

Mapping the Trail (10 min.) Use this question to move the group from acknowledging fears to confidence in what has been learned so far. Remind them that we will work together and that it will be fun to discover the Word as a group.

Teamwork (45 min.) Break into smaller groups so that people can participate in this and learn. If the group is too large, some will rely on the work of others.

The main theme of Hebrews is the supremacy of Christ and how his work on the cross replaces the old covenant. The Jews reading this might have been tempted to combine their Jewish sacrificial system with their newfound Christianity. The writer wants to avoid this, teaching them that Christ is the focus of faith. He also wants to encourage his readers because they are facing trials and possible persecution.

The type of literature is "epistle." Hebrews does not have all the normal structural components seen in many of the Epistles. Mostly it contains the body of the letter. A study Bible can give some additional background. You might also consult a Bible dictionary under "Hebrews" for more information to prepare for the meeting.

In Hebrews 2:5-9, Psalm 8:4-6 is quoted. Note the poetry used: verse 6 is synonymous parallelism and verses 7-8 is climactic parallelism.

The writer applies David's words here to Jesus, even though this is not a prophecy about the Christ. Jesus is the representative human in his incarnation and "the one in who man's appointed destiny will be fully realized" *(NIV Study Bible)*. Jesus is the ultimate human—the God-man—in whom we place our trust. He identified with us in life and death and became the sacrifice for our sin.

Hebrews 8:8-12 is a prophecy from Jeremiah 31:31-34. Jeremiah had already prophesied that Israel would spend seventy years in captivity (Jeremiah 25:8-15). Now he was directed by God to give them hope that God would restore them to the land and redeem them from their Babylonian captors. Jeremiah 30—31 is dedicated to their restoration and to God's renewed relationship with them ("So you will be my people, and I will be your God," 30:22).

This provides hope to the Hebrews, reminding them of the new covenant promised by God and how he had fulfilled part of the prophecy by bringing the people back from Babylon. But there was a spiritual part to the new covenant promise that was fulfilled in Christ. The new covenant has spiritual ramifications for Israel as they put God's laws in their hearts, not simply on stone tablets like the Ten Commandments. Now the writer wants people to realize the relationship they have as believing Jewish Christians, partakers of the new covenant in Christ. Thus there is a comparison in how God acted by returning Israel and Judah from bondage and how he is able to bring all people back from "bondage" to sin if they will trust Christ.

In Hebrews 9:11-15 it is clear that the Old Testament sacrificial system was inferior to the supreme sacrifice by Christ. People had to keep offering the sacrifices of bulls and goats because, ultimately, they did not cleanse sin (review Hebrews 10:1-14). Christ's blood is the supreme cleansing agent for our sin.

In Hebrews 12:4-11 readers are challenged to be disciplined, and the writer appeals to Proverbs 3:11-12 in verses 5-6. The writer makes an appeal to wisdom. If human fathers discipline sons and daughters whom they love, shouldn't God, whose love exceeds theirs, discipline his children as well? In this case the writer asks them to view their hardships as discipline from God that will produce spiritual fruit in their lives. The Hebrews, like us, struggled with sin. We are tempted and challenged. But we must take heart. When we are disciplined for our sin, we should see it as love from a heavenly Father who wants us to grow in holiness and maturity.

▲ **Reaching the Summit (5 min.)** Encourage your group members with all that has been learned. This book of the Bible integrates so many unique forms of literature and is a good example of why it is important to study what we have over the last few sessions. Help them remember that parables were studied as well. Encourage them to read some from Matthew 13 this week, for example, if they want to apply what they learned.

Read Hebrews 10:24-25 and encourage them to memorize it. It's a great verse to encourage gathering as a church or as a small group. Take a few minutes to celebrate what has been learned and affirm various members who may have found this quite challenging.

Next Session (10 min.) Encourage the group to study another book in the Bible 101 series or another study. An evening or weekend fun time, celebration or extended prayer meeting will be a healthy break from the last six meetings. Decide together what to do.

Close in Prayer (10 min.) Read Hebrews 12:28-29, and use it as a reference point for your prayer time. Remember to pray for group needs and concerns. Invite your group to express thanksgiving and worship, and take time to meet specific needs.